Original title:
Shadows of the Sycamore

Copyright © 2025 Creative Arts Management OÜ
All rights reserved.

Author: Theodore Sinclair
ISBN HARDBACK: 978-1-80567-173-2
ISBN PAPERBACK: 978-1-80567-472-6

Symphony of the Silent Woods

In the woods where critters play,
A squirrel dances, bright and gay.
The trees chuckle, branches sway,
As whispers float and join the fray.

An owl hoots a silly tune,
While rabbits hop beneath the moon.
The crickets chirp, in perfect sync,
As raccoons plot, with eyes that blink.

Frogs join in, with croaks so loud,
They form a band, the forest crowd.
With giggles hidden in each sound,
Nature's jesters all around.

A deer prances, but trips on moss,
Her friends all chuckle, they're at a loss.
Yet in this dance of whimsy grand,
The woods play on, a merry band.

The Dappled Dance of Branches

In sunlit flickers, branches sway,
They jiggle and wiggle, what a play!
Squirrels bust out their best moves,
While the leaves laugh and groove.

A gentle breeze starts the show,
Branches twist and bend, oh so slow!
A dance-off against the whistling air,
Who knew trees had such flair?

Secrets Cradled in Bark

Rusty whispers cling to thick limbs,
In the crevices lie tales, quite whims!
A woodpecker knows all the goss,
Tapping secrets that are hard to toss.

Knots in wood, a mystery brew,
Like old folks laughing at things they knew.
With a chuckle and a quirky grin,
The bark shares stories, let's dive in!

Veils of Evening Hues

As daylight dims, colors become bold,
The branches don outfits of gold.
A raccoon struts in twilight's grace,
Wearing shadows like a cozy lace.

Crickets start their buzzing song,
While owls hoot, playing along.
Under night's playful disguise,
Even the moon can't hide its surprise!

Beneath the Old Tree's Embrace

Cradled deep in its leafy bed,
A multitude of antics are spread.
A snail in boots takes a leisurely crawl,
While nearby ants host a grand ball.

The wise old tree spills giggles and charms,
Inviting creatures to all its arms.
Under its watch, no one's ever bored,
In its warm hug, laughter is stored!

Whispers Beneath the Canopy

Under leaves so green and wide,
A squirrel's chatter, full of pride.
He steals a nut with crafty flair,
And blames the bird for his despair.

Sunlight dances, tickles knees,
A rabbit giggles in the breeze.
With acorns bouncing, laughter rings,
Nature dons her jester's wings.

Echoes of the Forgotten Grove

In a grove where stories dwell,
A bear performs his stand-up well.
His jokes are fierce, yet hearts they win,
As trees laugh hard, their bark worn thin.

A raccoon steals the spotlight's glow,
With tales of treasures, big and low.
The owls hoot, they're quite a crowd,
As laughter echoes, bright and loud.

Twilight among Dappled Leaves

As twilight paints the sky so red,
A frog declares he's king, instead.
He croaks his crown, a royal halt,
While fireflies join in Jericho waltz.

The crickets chirp a tune so spry,
"Dance with us!" they cheerfully cry.
In this twilight, joy takes flight,
Nature laughs away the night.

Secrets Cradled in the Boughs

Within branches, secrets fly,
A wise old owl, he winks an eye.
With stories spun from ancient times,
He blabs the punchlines, drop the rhymes.

The raccoons plot a nightly tease,
While porcupines just giggle, please.
Nature's chaos, all in play,
In this wooded cabaret.

Ghosts of Autumn Winds

Leaves dance like spirits, they swirl and glide,
Whispering secrets, where mischief can hide.
Squirrels in chase, with acorns in tow,
Laughing at branches, that sway to and fro.

Pumpkins are juggling, on porches they sit,
While goblins skip past, in a brisk little fit.
Corn stalks are gossiping, what tales do they weave?
In the breeze, they chuckle, as if they believe.

Silhouettes in the Gloaming

Figures in twilight, they shuffle and shake,
Trying to blend in, for nighttime's sake.
Cats on a mission, with noses so bright,
Plotting their antics, beneath stars of white.

A raccoon in boots, struts down the lane,
While owls from the treetops hoot back in disdain.
The moon takes a peek, like a kid on the hood,
Laughing at creatures up to no good.

Branches Holding Silent Stories

Twisted trunk tales, of who climbed too high,
A crow wears a crown, as he caws from the sky.
Winds weave a riddle, that dances on air,
Tickling the leaves, with a playful flair.

Nutty debates, on who gets the last seed,
A family of chipmunks, with merry mischief, indeed.
Branches are tying, a pirate's old rope,
Adventures retraced, as they swing, twist, and mope.

Memories Etched in Green

Time's tender fingers, brush soft on the grass,
Where snapshots of laughter, flutter and pass.
A picnic's old blanket, now tattered and stained,
Tells tales of feasts, in the sun uncontained.

Frogs form a band, in the cool evening mist,
Croaking a symphony, nobody's missed.
The fireflies blink, showing off their best,
While crickets compose, a night-toontown fest.

Beneath the Arching Limbs

Squirrels in suits, they strut with flair,
Chasing each other without a care.
Acorns are treasures, oh what a find,
Nutty negotiations, they're one of a kind.

Birds in the branches all sing their tune,
While rabbits hold court beneath the moon.
Conversations of carrots, with giggles and glee,
In the shade of large leaves, wild and free!

Stories Haunting the Forest

Once a raccoon, tried to make a cake,
Found some old berries, oh what a mistake!
The bear in the corner just rolls with a sigh,
"That's not how you bake!" he lets out a cry.

Eerie tales linger as shadows do play,
With whispers of mischief that giggle away.
A fox dressed in stripes, claims it's all just a joke,
But the owl on the branch says, "That's no way to poke!"

A Tapestry of Twilit Whispers

Dancing moonbeams hit the ground,
Where mischief and giggles abound.
A hedgehog in glasses reads tales by the light,
While owls play cards, what a marvelous sight!

Crickets in chorus, they hum a soft tune,
With fireflies flashing like stars in June.
The froggy MC croaks beats on a stone,
While raccoons are rapping, they're never alone!

Sunlit Reveries Amidst the Branches

Under the sun, where the giggles thrive,
Mice in top hats, oh how they jive!
A parade of critters, a wondrous display,
With a dance-off planned for a glorious day.

The breezes bring laughter, they swirl and twine,
As the trees chuckle softly, oh so divine.
Adventures in sunlight, where nothing can stop,
From a dapper old snail with a lollipop!

The Traces of Nature's Breath

A squirrel danced without a care,
He spun around, caught the evening air.
A breeze tickled the playful tree,
While grass blades giggled, 'Come and see!'

The brook chimed in, with a giddy song,
As if it knew where the giggles belong.
It's nature's joke, a whimsical jest,
When every leaf is put to the test.

Enchanted Conversations among the Leaves

Two leaves held a chat, so cheeky and bold,
One claimed to wear a dress of pure gold.
The other just chuckled, 'That's quite a tale!'
'At least I'm not stuck, like a ship in a gale!'

The wind chimed in, with a hearty laugh,
'They've spun more tales than a wild giraffe!'
Meanwhile, the branches swayed with delight,
As nature enjoyed such a comical sight.

The Humming of Silhouetted Dreams

A cricket crooned to the moon so bright,
His legs a-tapping, what a funny sight!
The night winked back, a playful tease,
As dragonflies danced in the gentle breeze.

Each shadow chuckled, slipping and sliding,
As owls hooted, their laughter colliding.
In the twilight glow, dreams took their flight,
With giggles that echoed throughout the night.

Leaves as Pages of Forgotten Tales

On a sunny day, leaves whispered a plot,
Where squirrels were heroes, and humans forgot.
A tale of acorns, all shiny and round,
That rolled and hid without making a sound.

As seasons turned, the stories grew loud,
Each rustling leaf drawing in a crowd.
Filled with punchlines, the branches swayed,
Creating a laughter, unafraid and unfrayed.

The Chronicle of Quiet Hours

In the stillness, cats plot their schemes,
While squirrels chase dreams of nutty teams.
Waltzing leaves giggle in the breeze,
As bunnies wear hats made of dandelion seas.

Pillows of moss whisper soft lullabies,
As frogs recite jokes under a moonlit guise.
Every twig snaps like a punchline bright,
Nature's comedy plays till the dawn's first light.

Where Light Meets the Lattice

Sunbeams tickle the sleepy grass,
While shadows dance, quite the witty class.
Breezes crack jokes, laughter in the air,
The flowers nod along, without a care.

Overhead, birds chirp in a chorus grand,
Their tweets might just be jokes, unplanned.
The lattice of leaves frames a playful show,
As giggles ricochet from below.

The Language of Fall's Embrace

Crisp air whispers tales from the trees,
As pumpkins wear smiles, nothing to tweeze.
Dancing acorns tumble with a spree,
While ghosts in whites laugh, carefree.

Sweaters emerge from their summer nap,
As children delight in a crunching map.
Leaves toss and turn in a colorful jest,
Nature's own riddle, a seasonal quest.

Nature's Ink on the Forest Floor

Fallen leaves ink stories of the past,
As critters discuss which nuts will last.
A toad taps two-step, quite the charmer,
While critters debate who's the true farmer.

Mushrooms peek out, with their silly hats,
While wise old owls wink at the spats.
In the forest's nook, humor takes flight,
Each quirk a reminder of nature's delight.

Murmurs Under a Leafy Dome

Underneath the branches wide,
A squirrel plots with glee inside.
He gathers nuts with quite a flair,
While birds chirp jokes, without a care.

The leaves above shiver and shake,
As if they're laughing at the mistake.
A chipmunk trips, what a silly sight,
And all the critters cheer in delight.

Rabbits hop with a rhythmic groove,
While shadows dance, trying to prove.
That nature's comedy never ends,
As whispers tease and light descends.

In this leafy realm, laughter reigns,
With every rustle, joy contains.
So if you wander, stop and hear,
The chuckles of creatures, far and near.

The Hidden Heart of the Wood

In the wood where secrets dwell,
The mushrooms giggle, casting spells.
A raccoon dons a paper hat,
And asks the owls where's the snack at?

The trees exchange their gossip keen,
About the critters, skipping green.
A fox shows off his acrobats,
While hedgehogs play with fancy hats.

The sunlight sprays like champagne fizz,
While laughter dances, all a whizz.
Pretending to be wise and sage,
Yet none can act their proper age!

Amidst the greens, what joy we find,
With every twirl of playful bind.
So wander deep and hear the fun,
Where nature's pranks have just begun.

Hushed Conversations at Dusk

As twilight settles, whispers bloom,
A hedgehog frets in his cozy room.
"Did you hear what the owl said?
Brought the whole forest a bedspread!"

The crickets chirp in rhythmic rhyme,
While fireflies flash; a dance in time.
A babbling brook just can't contain,
A joke about a fish in the rain!

Amidst the stars, the creatures blend,
Sharing tales, where laughter transcends.
The owls nod knowingly, wise and sly,
As, "Who-hoo," echoes a merry sigh.

In shadows deep, the chuckles swell,
With every breeze, life's stories tell.
So linger here, and you will see,
The joy that lives in mystery.

The Dance of Light and Shade

Where the sun dapples on the ground,
A mischievous bunny leaps around.
He twirls and spins with boundless cheer,
While nearby whispers tickle the ear.

Squirrels clutch acorns like fine wine,
Offering gifts to the playful pine.
The shadows giggle, revealing their tricks,
As the ants have a party with little picks.

Light and dark weave their playful game,
Chasing each other, never the same.
The bushes hum, with secrets to share,
"Did you see the fox? He's late for a dare!"

So in this theater of nature's design,
Every moment, a jest divine.
Join the dance, let laughter ignite,
With the spirit of woods, oh so bright!

The Embrace of Twilight

The sun took a bow, it's time to depart,
As crickets tune up, they play from the heart.
The squirrels in tuxedos, all dance on a limb,
While fireflies gossip, their lights growing dim.

A raccoon in shades, he's up for a snack,
He sneaks through the grass, with a curious clack.
The moon winks down, it's a night full of cheer,
In this twilight embrace, let's all raise a beer!

Whispers Beneath the Canopy

Underneath leafy tales, the breeze has a plan,
With a tickle of wind, it sweeps through the land.
The owls crack jokes with a hoot and a clap,
While rabbits, in giggles, fall into a nap.

The branches are bending to hear a good pun,
As shadows all chuckle, they're having such fun.
The worms play charades, just a wiggle or two,
And the leaves sway along, saying, "We get you!"

The Fragrance of Fading Days

As daylight dips low, a scent fills the air,
A whiff of absurdity, drifting everywhere.
The flowers in bloom start to blush just a bit,
Gossiping sweet tales that make no sense, fit?

The bees start to hum their slightly off tune,
While daisies debate if it's day or it's noon.
The perfume of laughter gets stronger each hour,
In this fragrant confusion, we all feel the power!

The Memory of a Sunlit Glen

In a glen where the sun paints a dance on the grass,
Blades tickle each toe, making moments amass.
The butterflies chuckle in colors so bold,
While ladybugs ponder on secrets untold.

The bunnies play tag with their floppy big ears,
While laughter from waterfalls echoes in cheers.
With sunshine as confetti, the day rolls away,
In this memory's light, we all choose to stay!

Beneath the Verdant Veil

In the grove where squirrels play,
Leaves whisper secrets, come what may.
A raccoon dons a dapper hat,
As chubby worms dance, 'round and fat.

With nature's giggles all around,
Frogs sing silly songs, profound.
A ladybug performs a jig,
While ants parade, all neat and big.

Beneath the canopy, joy is rife,
A tree stump holds the tales of life.
The breeze will tease and tickle too,
As leaves engage in hearty brew.

Beneath the green, not quite so shy,
A gopher tells a joke, oh my!
And butterflies, in laughter, sway,
As woodland friends join in the play.

Threads of Life Intertwined

A spider spins a web of glee,
While gossip flows amongst the tree.
A raccoon swipes a donut treat,
While chipmunks stumble on their feet.

In this realm of tangled fun,
Where every branch has stories spun,
The bumblebee, with plucky pride,
Stirs up some cheer with every glide.

An acorn hat atop a snail,
As toadstools shade a wobbly trail.
The laughter of the leaves, a tune,
Beneath the watchful eye of moon.

Those roots are friends, so deep and tight,
In this merry, woodland fight.
Every twig a joke is told,
As laughter weaves through threads of gold.

Secrets in the Wind's Caress

The wind reveals a tale to tell,
Of how the fox thought he could spell.
He scratched his head, then gave a grin,
As birds chirped loudly, 'You can't win!'

With every gust, the stories fly,
A dandelion's wish goes shy.
The grasshoppers, in a high-pitched choir,
Leap and shout like little fire.

The secrets dance on breezy beams,
While flowers giggle in their dreams.
A squirrel with shades, so suave and cool,
Teases the birds who skip from school.

In whispers soft, the wind confides,
With acorns rolling, laughter rides.
As nature plays her merry game,
The woods erupt with joy, no shame.

Woodland Oaths Under Moonlight

A raccoon swears to clean his plate,
While owls hoot at a squirrel's fate.
The moonlight shines on critter quests,
As laughter bubbles from their chests.

With giggly vows beneath the light,
They promise snacks will be just right.
The porcupine boasts a comfy quill,
While fireflies dance on dreamy hill.

Beneath the watchful stars so bright,
Those woodland friends declare a night.
A river sings a croaky tune,
As frogs join in, beneath the moon.

With every layer of leafy cheer,
They sip the nectar of the year.
In woodland oaths, no room for gloom,
Each critter laughs, as dreams consume.

A Canopy of Dreams

Underneath the leafy green,
Squirrels dance, a funny scene.
Chasing tails and nuts galore,
Who knew trees could hold such lore?

A raccoon snickers, pulls a prank,
While birds debate, then form a rank.
Laughter echoes, laughter loud,
In this leafy, leafy crowd.

Frogs croak jokes in silly tune,
As fireflies begin to swoon.
The breeze whispers a silly rhyme,
In this enchanted place, just sublime.

The Stillness in the Grove

In the grove, a whisper stirs,
A gopher laughs, and then it purrs.
While beetles march, all in a line,
Proclaiming victory—purely divine!

The owl hoots with a knowing wink,
As chipmunks gather, gossip and think.
With nutty stories passed around,
The comedy of critters is profound.

A mouse wearing oversized shoes,
Jumps from a stump, is it a ruse?
In the stillness, giggles creep,
As nature holds its breath, a peep.

Beneath the Rustic Boughs

Beneath the branches, all askew,
A badger slips, right on cue.
He tumbles down with quite a flair,
Swearing he was never there!

A crow mocks with a caw so bright,
As rabbits hop in pure delight.
They juggle acorns, such a sight,
A woodsy circus, oh what a fright!

The wind joins in with a giggle or two,
As flowers sway like they agree too.
In this rustic theater full of fun,
Nature laughs until the day is done.

Twilight's Lament in the Woods

As twilight falls, a glow so sweet,
The critters gather for a treat.
A wise old tortoise spills some tea,
While dancing moths sip merrily.

The fireflies flicker, stars on the ground,
While rabbits bounce, making no sound.
The trees sway with a giggly tune,
While crickets chirp beneath the moon.

A hedgehog starts a joke or two,
That has the crowd all laughing blue.
In this twilight, everything's bright,
Fun and folly dance in the night.

Veil of the Leafy Haven

In a park where laughter flows,
Frogs hold court, with silly prose.
A squirrel wears a dapper hat,
Chasing bugs in a playful spat.

The breeze laughs, a teasing friend,
Whispers secrets that never end.
Beneath the tree, ants conspire,
Plotting games that don't require.

Dandelion fluff takes flight,
Tickles noses, pure delight.
Grasshoppers leap, a daring show,
As butterflies dance to and fro.

Sunlight dapples, games ignite,
Nature's fun, a pure delight.
With every rustle, giggles grow,
In this leafy world, joy will flow.

Stories Carried by the Wind

Whispers ride on zephyr's breath,
Tales of mischief, life, and death.
A leaf spins down, a daring dive,
Wishing glasses help us thrive.

The wind chuckles, oh so sly,
Taking naps in clouds up high.
Crickets play their nightly tune,
While owls hoot at the glowing moon.

Dancing daisies bold and bright,
Tickled by the stars at night.
The trees sway, join the dance,
In this realm, we take our chance.

Come closer, feel the waltz of fate,
Time to giggle, time to wait.
For every breeze that comes and goes,
Tells a story that often flows.

Fragments of Light in the Dark

Moonlight plays on squirrel trails,
While fireflies tell glowing tales.
In the dark, a mouse sings low,
Echoes of a midnight show.

Owl's wink, a cheeky tease,
What's not to love? Just feel the breeze!
Beneath the stars, a laugh takes flight,
As shadows dance in the soft night light.

Tall grass hides the wild and free,
Chasing giggles like the sea.
With every flicker, dreams embark,
To chase the light amidst the dark.

Join the jesters of the night,
Where laughter glows, and hearts feel light.
For in this glow of nature's spark,
Joy awaits, in every arc.

The Hidden Heart of the Forest

In the woods where secrets dwell,
A fox tells stories, casting a spell.
The mushrooms chuckle, dressed in spots,
Join the giggles, connect the dots.

A raccoon pranks with mischievous flair,
While the trees gossip without a care.
Frogs on logs croak a funny beat,
Nature's jesters, never discreet.

Sunbeams peer through leaves so lush,
Creating laughter in the hush.
Every rustle, a playful tease,
With whispers carried on the breeze.

So tread lightly on the forest floor,
Join the jest in this green encore.
For in this heart where laughter's stored,
Every moment becomes adored.

Beneath the Stillness of Ancient Branches

Squirrels in suits, they hold a debate,
Arguing acorns until it's too late.
A raccoon on a swing, he's feeling so spry,
Loop-de-looping beneath the blue sky.

Leaves gossip softly, what secrets they keep,
Claiming the tree knows when to sleep.
A jester of nature stumbling around,
Tickling the roots with his shoes made of sound.

What's that noise? Just a card in a breeze,
It's quite the ruckus while dancing with ease.
The old tree chuckles, its bark bows in glee,
While birds plan a party, all merry and free.

Glimmers in the Gloom

In the evening light, a ghost wearing socks,
Tiptoes past owls, avoiding their clocks.
The fireflies giggle, they blink and they tease,
While frogs in bow ties hold court with great ease.

An old toad sings opera, what a funny sight,
His voice, but a croak, is a laugh in the night.
Crickets compete with their chirps for the throne,
Who knew insects could fight for a home loan?

The moon looks baffled, what's happening here?
A comedy show 'neath the sky so clear.
With each little twinkle and flutter of wings,
Laughter has blossomed, as nature sings.

Beneath the Whispering Leaves

A chattering rabbit pretends to be wise,
Holding court with the bugs, wearing glasses and ties.
The ladybugs laugh, they know he's a phony,
While foxes make plans for a dance at the crony.

The leaves are all chuckling, they sway to the tune,
As critters conspire to lighten the gloom.
What mischief they brew 'neath the branches so wide,
With a swirl and a twirl, they let humor glide.

And if you sit quiet, you might hear the fun,
With whispers of giggles beneath the warm sun.
Each rustle and ripple, a lesson so grand,
That nature is laughing; come join, take a stand!

The Enigmatic Dance of Twilight

The sun dips low, a mischievous thief,
Hiding in clouds, causing some disbelief.
As shadows stretch long, they trip on their toes,
Falling like laughter that nobody knows.

A mouse with a monocle grins from his spot,
Counting the stars; he's a lucky shot!
The bats wear their capes, swishing with flair,
While owls plot the pranks that they're bound to declare.

In the dim light, a dance party springs,
Each creature unwinds, showing off their wings.
With twirls and with flips, the moon takes a bow,
In twilight's embrace, they all chuckle somehow.

Rooted in Reverie

A tree in a hat, oh what a sight,
Branches swaying with all their might.
Birds chirp tunes, they sing with flair,
Dancing on leaves, without a care.

Squirrels argue over acorn stash,
Rolling around, making a splash.
The sun's a jester, casting a grin,
While shadows and laughter softly spin.

Chronicle of the Woven Light

A flicker of sun in a knotty weave,
Riddles of humor the branches conceive.
Breezes gossip as they tickle the bark,
Each leaf a word, brightening the dark.

A wise old owl, with spectacles perched,
Keeps notes of the pranks that nature has churched.
From swinging raccoons to leaping frogs,
This tale of whimsy, a dance with logs.

The Sigh of the Ancient Boughs

With a creak and a groan, the old limbs jest,
Telling tall tales, they never rest.
Bumblebees buzz like the town's loud gossip,
While sturdy roots offer a comical grip.

A breeze blows softly, rustles the leaves,
Echoing laughs that tickle and tease.
In a world so spry, with antics galore,
Even the insects can't help but roar.

In the Quiet of Falling Leaves

A dance of gold as they flutter down,
Each one a caper, a whirl, a frown.
Twirling and laughing through autumn's delight,
Nature's own show, a whimsical sight.

The ground's a canvas, splashes of cheer,
Creating a quilt that whispers near.
Little critters dive into the spree,
In a leaf pile party, come join and see!

The Pledge of Timeless Growth

In the park where tall trees sway,
A squirrel debates his acorn today.
He vows to plant it, oh what a feat,
But forgets where he buried his tasty treat.

Each leaf whispers secrets lost in the breeze,
While children run by with giggles and wheeze.
Promises echo in every small laugh,
As the world spins on a never-ending path.

Old roots gripping stories, they chuckle with glee,
As weathered bark holds their history.
Nature's a jester in a leafy crown,
With antics that never let laughter drown.

So here's to the growth that comes with some spice,
Where every misstep is a roll of the dice.
Let's plant our hopes, in this silly embrace,
And find joy in every strange place.

Fingerprints of Autumn Glow

Golden leaves dance in a playful sweep,
As chilly winds tease and make you leap.
A pumpkin rolls away, full of despair,
While a mischievous squirrel steals away with flair.

The sun dips low, like a tired old cat,
As children chase shadows dressed like a bat.
They trip on their laughter, fall into cheer,
Wrapped in the magic of this time of year.

Pies cool on windows, as aromas collide,
With all of our senses, the joy takes a ride.
But one too many bites, oh what a surprise,
As Grandma's secret recipe fills more than just pies.

Autumn's a party, where memories bloom,
With corny jokes booming from every room.
We raise our mugs, filled with cider galore,
And toast to the giggles, and always wanting more.

The Residue of a Moonlit Memory

Under a blanket of twinkling delight,
A raccoon put on a show in the night.
With wobbly steps, he danced on the grass,
His moonlit performances made all of us laugh.

Stars winked in rhythm, as crickets played tunes,
While shadows played tag, beneath cotton ball moons.
A moth tried to flirt, but got caught in a web,
With a spider as best friend, and no need to beg.

Nostalgia drapes softly like a warm fuzzy coat,
Where each small mishap is worth a good note.
Memories echo, with time's gentle nudge,
As laughter holds on, it'll never judge.

So let's keep those giggles that bubble and flow,
For life is a dance, in the moon's gentle glow.
Each starlit moment a chance to explore,
With memories lingering, who could want more?

The Canvas of the Dimming Sky

The canvas stretches wide with colors so bright,
As day's curtain falls, giving way to the night.
Dandelions drift like wishes afloat,
While the sun takes a bow in a tiny old boat.

Pinks and purples, all swirling in sight,
As fireflies buzz in a twinkling delight.
A child points in awe at this dazzling affair,
While a butterfly giggles and swirls through the air.

Clouds get creative, with shapes in the breeze,
A dog chases shadows with a playful tease.
In this show of colors and silly delight,
Even the crickets join in on the sight.

So let's paint our dreams on the night's canvas wide,
With laughter and wonder as our hearts' guide.
In life's funny gallery, every moment's a gift,
As the world spins on, we share each quirky lift.

When Light Fades into the Wood

As sunlight dips down low,
The squirrels start a show.
With acorns as their props,
They're dancing 'til it stops.

The trees begin to creak,
The owls are starting to peek.
A raccoon tells a joke,
While shadows play the cloak.

The breeze begins to sway,
With whispers on display.
A beetle sings a tune,
As laughter fills the gloom.

A fox joins in the fun,
Playing tag, on the run.
In twilight's gentle phase,
The critters play their plays.

Silhouettes Beneath the Moon

When the moon starts to rise,
Little critters improvise.
A badger spins a tale,
While owls hoot without fail.

Beneath the silver glow,
Funny shadows dance and flow.
A rabbit trips in fright,
Embracing the cool night.

The trees make faces grand,
While fireflies light the land.
A raccoon winks his eye,
Knowing it's all a lie.

Laughter fills the air,
Never shows a care.
With silliness so bright,
They jive into the night.

The Forgotten Ones of the Green Realm

In the forest, tales unfold,
Of creatures brave and bold.
But there's one silly chap,
Who thought he'd take a nap.

A turtle named McGee,
Dreamed of flying free.
He strapped a leaf to his shell,
And yelled, "I'll soar! What the hell!"

The ants all gathered 'round,
With laughter, they abound.
"Hey, slowpoke, just stand still,
You've got a different skill!"

So he sat, quite confused,
As his plans were abused.
In the realm where they dwell,
They love their stories well.

Whispers of Old Roots

Beneath the twisted limbs,
Where sunlight starts to dim,
Old roots have tales to spin,
With mischief tucked within.

A worm named Carl, so shy,
Claimed he could touch the sky.
He squiggled with great zest,
In search of his big quest.

The trees began to laugh,
At his squirmy, silly path.
They whispered soft and low,
"Carl, stay down here, you know!"

But Carl was quite determined,
Through laughter, he kept wormin'.
In the heart of the wood,
They cheered, as best they could.

Murmuring Hearts of the Grove

In the trees, the squirrels chatter,
Telling tales that make hearts flatter.
Rabbits racing, grasses sway,
Who knew the woods would play today?

Breezes tease with faux embrace,
Ticklish leaves, a playful race.
A woodpecker, all in glee,
Knocks a tune, just for me!

Mushrooms dance in funny hats,
Wiggly worms and chubby rats.
Nature giggles, can't you see?
A woodland jester, wild and free!

Underneath the dappled light,
Every bark sounds just so right.
In this grove, my heart can sing,
Where laughter's found in everything.

Sketches in the Dusk

As the sun dips low and sly,
Crickets start to croon and cry.
Fireflies flicker, brief and bright,
Sketching dreams in fading light.

The moon peeks in, a cheeky face,
Playing hide and seek with space.
Bats perform their evening ballet,
Flipping through the twilight play.

Mice in coats of velvet grey,
Join the frolic, hip-hip-hooray!
Even shadows find their voice,
In this whimsical choice.

Laughter echoes, soft and wide,
An echo of the twilight tide.
In the dusk, we find our fun,
As stars wink down, one by one.

The Cradle of Whispering Winds

Gusts of laughter swirl the trees,
Whispers bouncing on the breeze.
A dandelion's golden fluff,
Giggling all, it's never tough!

The brook chuckles, leaping stones,
With tiny fish in striped tones.
Hey there, turtle, what's the fuss?
Even snails are joining us!

The crickets hold a serenade,
While the sun plays peekaboo parade.
All the while, the daisies grin,
Knowing well the fun within.

In the cradle of night's embrace,
Every creature finds their place.
With winds that whisper, soft and free,
Join the laughter; come dance with me!

A Dance with the Diminished Light

Twilight weaves a playful song,
Where critters shimmy, clap along.
The shadows stretch, but they won't fall,
When nature's laughter rules them all!

A glow-worm leads the jitterbug,
While squirrels pull a sneaky shrug.
The fireflies join the twinkling reel,
In the air, there's joy to feel!

The groundhog's waltz is quite absurd,
Twirling 'round, it flips and spurred.
In the fading light's embrace,
All the creatures find their pace.

With every laugh in this brief night,
The world becomes a pure delight.
So come on, friends, let's join the spree,
In this dance of glee, just you and me!

The Resilience of Weathered Leaves

Cracked and chipping paint of green,
Dancing with the breeze, unseen.
With a rustle, they might complain,
But in their humor, they remain.

A squirrel climbs with all his might,
Flipping leaves left and right.
"Hold on tight!" he squeaks with glee,
Daring fate, as bold as can be.

Underfoot, they tap dance loud,
Creating laughter, gathering crowd.
Conversations stuck in the air,
Tales of summers, if you care.

As autumn paints them shades of fire,
They giggle as they rise and tire.
For no one can dispute their creed,
Laugh and fall, it is indeed!

Beneath the Old Tree's Gaze

Beneath the branches wide and wise,
The creatures plot with goofy eyes.
A rat wears glasses, reading a book,
While the crow gives scandalous looks.

"Who needs shade?" the rooster crows,
While trimming his feathers in rows.
The tree just chuckles, winds eventide,
As giggles flourish where they're denied.

Floating whispers dance in the air,
As fireside secrets get laid bare.
Even ants have stories to tell,
Of mischief and fun, they love so well.

Sudden wind blows, they laugh not cry,
As leaves twirl around, like kids in the sky.
A sight to see, an old tree's glee,
Underneath the sunny spree!

The Slow Weaving of Memories

In a tapestry of tangled dreams,
Thick and thin, or so it seems.
Stitching laughter, buttoned tight,
As memories twirl in evening light.

A kitten yawns and stretches wide,
On a thread of days, she takes a ride.
While grandpa grins, his stories spun,
Mighty yarns of when he was young.

They weave their tales with gentle paws,
Each stitch a giggle, a rightful pause.
With needles sharp and threads so bright,
They craft a quilt of delight.

Every fray holds laughter's scent,
Of silly jests and good intent.
As clouds drift softly out of sight,
The fabric's richer, in shared delight!

Hearth of the Muyetia

Gathered round the flickering glow,
Friends swap stories, deep and low.
A tune from the cat begins to play,
As folks burst into dance and sway.

Miss Mary's pie is charmingly round,
While Grandpa's jokes are renowned.
Each crumb a memory, sweet or sour,
In this cozy nook, laughter's power.

The fire crackles, sparks take flight,
As shadows join the dance tonight.
With antics bright, they hoot and laugh,
In a comedic, swirling half.

As twilight wraps its velvet cloak,
In every hearth, a charming joke.
With mugs raised high, they toast with cheer,
To the love we share, year after year!

The Gentle Sway of Time

In breezy dance, the branches wave,
As squirrels plot and misbehave.
With acorns dropping, what a sight,
The tree may giggle with delight.

The sunbeams tickle leaves above,
While birds compose their songs of love.
A gentle tease, the winds they make,
The trunk just sighs, "For goodness' sake!"

As seasons change and days go by,
The whispers rise, the laughter's high.
Old bark remembers all the fun,
With every day, a new pun spun.

The world beneath the leafy crown,
Is full of chuckles, upside down.
With twinkling eyes, it sways in glee,
In this grand game of hide and tree.

A Tangle of Roots and Dreams

Beneath the soil, the secrets hide,
With tangled roots, they swell with pride.
Each little worm a joyous friend,
In this confab, there's no end.

The toads all croak their witty lines,
While moles recount their wild designs.
Oh, what a ruckus down below,
As dreams sprout wings that flutter so!

The fallen leaves play hide and seek,
While nature shares a silly peek.
A dance of laughs, a whirling spin,
In tangled tales where laughs begin.

The roots entwine, a jolly show,
As laughter's echo starts to grow.
With every twist and playful dare,
Life's a circus, just stop and stare.

Noggin of the Noble Tree

With brainy bark, it holds the key,
To secrets of the bouncy spree.
Its gnarled face wears wisdom's grin,
A goofy sage that loves to spin.

The branches wave as if to say,
"Life's one big joke, come join the play!"
With every rustle, leaves connect,
In laughter's game, you're sure to expect.

It does a jig when breezes blow,
And tickles roots down low, you know.
The knobby knots, they chuckle too,
In this great comedy, all is true.

So gather near, and lend an ear,
For wisdom spoken, loud and clear.
The noble tree, with noggin wise,
Will share its anecdotes, so wise.

Testament of the Weathered Knots

In every gnarled and weathered twist,
Lies a tale that can't be missed.
With laughter rings and stories bright,
Each knot a wink in cozy light.

The echoes of the playful winds,
Whisper of joys, and old-time sins.
The tree holds court, with bark as throne,
Where nature shares its love, well-known.

As branches stretch to catch a dream,
In every leaf, a giggle gleams.
The wisdom written in the grain,
Is etched in joy, not just in pain.

The knots proclaim, in jest and cheer,
"Embrace the quirks, let out a tear!"
A testament to life's delight,
In every twist, a laugh ignites.

The Echoing Breath of the Woods

In the woods where squirrels play,
A raccoon rapped on my door today.
He waved his paw, said, "Let us feast!"
While birds threw crumbs, a wild beast.

The trees were giggling, it seemed quite clear,
With branches waving like they had a beer.
A deer in a tutu danced on the grass,
As mushrooms chuckled, brought forth a laugh.

Frogs in bow ties croaked their best tunes,
While fireflies waltzed beneath the moons.
A raccoon rolled over, slipped on a twig,
Getting up dizzied, doing a jig.

So here I wander, a smile on my face,
In a merry woodland, a comical place.
Where critters plot the night's jolly fate,
Under the trees, it's never too late.

Guardians of the Leafy Realm

The owls in robes, wise and quite sly,
Play poker by night, where stars flicker by.
Squirrels act as their cheerful hands,
Passing nuts while obeying the plans.

Rabbits don capes, they jump with delight,
Whispering secrets 'neath the pale light.
A raccoon tries hard not to smirk,
As turtles debate all the hard work.

The fox brings donuts, a tasty surprise,
Claiming they're magic, you just have to try!
While the badgers, with hats made of leaves,
Plot absurd jokes that nobody believes.

All kingdom of green, with laughter to share,
In cleverly woven, everyday flair.
With giggles and snickers, they guard their domain,
In leafy havens, delight will remain.

The Ghost of Summer's Breath

When summer fades, the breeze gets a chill,
Ghosts float around, making mischief and thrill.
One snatched my sandwich right out of my hand,
As I chased it down through the golden sand.

There were whispers of laughter, behind every tree,
A playful spirit, thought it'd tease me.
With shadows that danced under the sun,
This ghost loved hide-and-seek, oh what fun!

It painted the leaves in hues far and wide,
Then waved at the sunlight, a playful ride.
It stole all the ice cream, then dashed away,
Laughing just like a child at play.

So here I stand, with crumbs on my face,
Thankful for the ghost found in this place.
For joy brings laughter, like a warm embrace,
In the summer's breath, here's a lovely trace.

Twilight's Gentle Caress

As dusk falls softly, colors intertwine,
With giggles of frogs, and bats so divine.
Fireflies organize a dance in the air,
As crickets recite their songs without care.

The trees join the fun, swaying with glee,
While owls hoot softly with cultured decree.
The hedgehogs are gossiping, tails all a-fluff,
Balloons made of leaves — the night gets tough!

A fox with a crown claims to be the king,
While raccoons in tuxedos refute this bling.
The moon rolls her eyes, amused at the scene,
As stars throw confetti, oh what a routine!

In twilight's embrace, all worries retreat,
With laughter and joy, life's sweet little treat.
In the darkening woods, friendships ignite,
In the playful hush of the fading light.

Tales Woven in the Twilight

In twilight's glow, the critters prance,
A raccoon dons his silly pants.
He twirls and twists with all his flair,
And lands a dance without a care.

The owl squints with a look so sly,
As fireflies buzz and flit on by.
He gives a wink, a secret shared,
In laughter's grip, the night is bared.

A squirrel, too, joins in the fun,
Balancing acorns, one by one.
But oh, he slips; what a grand sight,
As nuts take flight in sheer delight!

When evening fades, the giggles linger,
Each creature waves with a joyous finger.
For in the night, with laughter bright,
The woodland's heart feels just right.

Beneath the Enchanted Branches

Under the leaves, a badger grins,
He jokes about his chubby fins.
A hedgehog laughs, rolled tight in ball,
"This isn't how I planned to sprawl!"

The branches sway in gentle glee,
As squirrels plot a comedy spree.
In every nook, a giggle grows,
With bouncing friends and childish prose.

An ant spills tea, an epic blunder,
Two ants collide, oh what a thunder!
The tea's on them, like sticky glue,
As they shake off their brew anew.

When moonlight spills, their laughter flies,
With winks and jests under starry skies.
Beneath the boughs, all worries cease,
In nature's mirth, there's purest peace.

Whispers Beneath the Canopy

Beneath the boughs, the stories soar,
A chipmunk sings; we crave for more.
He slides down roots with comical flair,
    Creating giggles that fill the air.

A turtle trips, so slow, so sly,
He raises a leg and shoots for the sky.
With every tumble, the crowd erupts,
As laughter spreads, and frowns are plucked.

A fox with flair brings snacks to share,
But serves them up with a twirling flair.
    His juggling act is quite the sight,
        As berries fly into the night.

In rustling leaves, the jokes take flight,
For woodland friends, it's pure delight.
Their whispers dance with the evening breeze,
    In symphonies of mirth, they tease.

Echoes of Twilight Leaves

In twilight hues, the laughter swells,
A rabbit shares his carrot tales.
He hops around on oversized feet,
And shows off moves to a funky beat.

The raccoon chimes in, a trickster bold,
With stories of treasure, bright and old.
He swipes a hat, declares it grand,
While all the critters clap and stand.

A bear arrives, so clumsy and sweet,
He stumbles over his zeal to greet.
With every bump, the giggles grow,
As he joins in the show, so slow.

Under the stars, the humor beams,
As creatures weave their funny dreams.
In echoes sweet, the night retreats,
With laughter shared, all life completes.

Beneath the Brooding Boughs

Beneath the branches stout and wide,
A squirrel sneaks with nutty pride.
He dances left, then hops on right,
Thinking he's a furry knight.

The branches shake with muffled laughs,
As worms throw darts at tiny drafts.
A giggling breeze climbs up the tree,
While birds just chirp, 'Hey, look at me!'

With secret codes and acorn plans,
The critters form their little clans.
A game of tag on leave-strewn floor,
Each chase a giggle, never a bore.

At dusk, they gather, tales unfold,
Of leafy adventures brave and bold.
Beneath the boughs where fun reigns free,
There's mischief hidden, can't you see?

Cradle of Nature's Sighs

In the cradle where the breezes play,
A ladybug claims her café.
With tiny cups and wings so bright,
She serves up pollen, sparkles in flight.

A mouse with aspirations grand,
Dreams of holding a rock band.
He strums a twine with pewter clap,
While frogs croak back a raucous rap.

The moon peeks down, a merry fan,
As crickets conduct with graceful hand.
Each note a chuckle; oh, what a show!
As fireflies dance in the night's glow.

This cradle hums with witty glee,
A stage where all are meant to be.
With laughter swirling, nature sighs,
In this delight, the heart just flies.

The Pulse of High Canopy

Where the leaves whisper and twirl about,
A jumble of critters start to shout.
A raccoon juggles acorns high,
While doing flips, oh my, oh my!

With nimble paws, a lizard darts,
Trying to play the fool's fine arts.
A dance of light on velvet leaves,
As everyone giggles and waits for eaves.

A parrot squawks an epic tale,
While shadows wiggle, tickle's the trail.
The dance floor beats with feathery flair,
As insects buzz, the joy fills the air.

In this high realm where giggles thrive,
Nature's charm is very much alive.
The pulse of play, a vibrant spree,
In laughter stitched through each green tree.

A Magician's Fairytale in Green

A magician waves from boughs so lush,
With tricks that make the flowers blush.
He pulls a rabbit from thin air,
While crickets tweet, 'We won't despair!'

With every flourish, butterflies dart,
As magic dances, pulling hearts.
A cat performs a juggling act,
But fumbles fish—it's quite the fact!

He conjures dreams from starlit leaps,
As nature stirs, and laughter seeps.
His hat is full of nature's cheer,
While all the woodland creatures cheer.

In this fairytale of leafy schemes,
Reality bends, and whimsy beams.
A joke, a grin, a riddle keen,
All in the realm of vibrant green.

The Heartbeat of Amber Leaves

The breeze it tickles, just for fun,
A dance of leaves as bright as sun.
Squirrels plotting snacks on high,
   Chasing dreams that flutter by.

A bashful branch plays peek-a-boo,
While acorns drop like morning dew.
The laughter echoes through the boughs,
   As critters feast and take their bows.

With every rustle, tales unfold,
Of mischief done and treasures bold.
A scene of whimsy etched in green,
Where every moment's fit for a queen.

So come and join this leafy jest,
Where nature's pranks are truly best.
In amber hues, the heartbeats sing,
   Of silly games this season brings.

The Lullaby of Swaying Branches

Under the moon, the branches sway,
Whispering secrets in child's play.
A raccoon dons a silly hat,
And dances jigs with nary a spat.

The glowworms waltz in evening air,
While fireflies giggle, unaware.
A little owl hoots a tune,
As shadows twist beneath the moon.

Each leaf a note, a gentle sound,
Melodies in the darkness found.
Swaying branches, arms uplift,
Granting wishes, a playful gift.

So drift along, let laughter grow,
In nature's lullaby, soft and slow.
Where merry dreams blend with night,
And every star brings pure delight.

The Legacy of Eclipsed Sundown

As daylight fades, the pranks begin,
With crickets chirping, loud and thin.
A bat zooms by with a playful shriek,
Making grand leaps, oh so chic!

The clouds wear hats of deepening grey,
While sunlight slips, it starts to play.
A rabbit hops with shoes too big,
Displaying moves that are quite a fig.

With each twinkle in darkening skies,
The fireflies join in holiday highs.
Whispers float from trees up high,
As owls steal glances while passing by.

The legacy lives where laughter flows,
In twilight wonder where mischief grows.
With every dusk, a new tale's spun,
Of joy and jest until day is done.

Enigmas in the Dusty Glade

In a hidden nook, where secrets crawl,
A hedgehog's giggle breaks the thrall.
Amidst the ferns, a riddle lays,
Of pranks and games, oh what a craze!

The sunbeams play hide-and-seek,
While shadows run away in squeaks.
A wise old tortoise grins and sighs,
With twinkling eyes, oh what a prize!

A maze of paths where whispers roam,
Every twist feels like coming home.
Nature's puzzle, a laugh to find,
Here, every heart leaves worries behind.

So wander through this breezy spot,
Where whimsical wonders surely trot.
Embrace the joy held in the glade,
Savor the smiles that life has made.

Nightfall in the Canopy

As dusk drapes on the leafy scene,
The squirrels plot, devising their scheme.
With acorns tucked in tiny paws,
They leap and bound without a pause.

Crickets chirp their nightly song,
While fireflies dance, but not for long.
An owl hoots jokes to the silent night,
As stars twinkle in pure delight.

The raccoons don their masks with flair,
Waltzing through shadows without a care.
The moon grins wide at their carefree spree,
Chasing away worries like an old decree.

Echoes of Green Dreams

In the green glades where giggles burst,
Breezes tease, as if rehearsed.
A rabbit juggles carrots with glee,
While beetles breakdance by the old tree.

The turtles race, though it's quite slow,
Their enthusiastic cheers begin to grow.
With every laugh, the leaves sway too,
Join in the fun, their rustling crew.

Hopping frogs start a croaky band,
With frogs on keys, we can't understand.
Nature's party lasts through the night,
As stars become the disco light.

When the Sun Falls Silent

When the sun takes its final bow,
The garden prepares for a nighttime wow.
A hedgehog rolls in laughter's embrace,
While snickering foxes claim their space.

The garden gnomes begin their dance,
With wobbly moves and strange prance.
Mice gather round, sipping on cheese,
As fireflies twinkle, putting us at ease.

Crickets serve as the evening's band,
With rhythms wild and slightly unplanned.
As laughter echoes through the moonlit glade,
We find joy in the games we've played.

The Embrace of Evening's Grasp

As dusk envelops with a playful tease,
Frogs in tuxedos hop with ease.
Underneath the boughs, giggles abound,
Where night finds mischief, joy is found.

Bats perform aerial tricks high above,
While owls whisper tales of nighttime love.
A raccoon family seeks shiny treasure,
In baskets of laughter, beyond all measure.

The paths of the forest weave strange tales,
With every prank beneath the veils.
As evening paints the world with grace,
The critters share a chuckle's embrace.

Memories Written in Bark

Scratching letters on rough skin,
A squirrel laughs at my chagrin.
I carved my heart, it came out wrong,
The tree just chuckled, 'Sing your song!'

Raccoons read my love notes at night,
With tiny paws, they giggle in delight.
A love so deep it left a mark,
Yet, here I stand, still in the dark!

Old maple whispers, 'Try again!'
I brought a sharp knife, and I made a friend.
But all my words now sprout and grow,
In tangled roots, they twist and flow.

So if you hear a tree chuckle near,
Beware—your secrets will disappear!
With every laugh, they move and sway,
Trace your memories—better find a way!

Twilight's Soft Embrace

Under fading rays of light,
The insects spin in dizzy flight.
A firefly winks with all its might,
'Dance with me, it's party night!'

The moon peeks through, a cheeky sprite,
'You're too old for this—quite right!'
But here we twirl in giggles bright,
Knees knocking, it's quite a sight!

Napping cats join in the fun,
Rolling over, their hearts have won.
With each pounce, the fairies run,
In twilight's glow, we all are one!

So gather close, as night sings loud,
In this embrace, we're all so proud.
For laughter be the sweetest sound,
And joy in twilight can be found!

The Dance of Morning Dews

Waking up to a sparkling show,
Tiny droplets that gleam below.
They laugh and hop, as breezes flow,
In waltzing grass, the dew drops glow.

'Come join us!' call the leaves so spry,
As bees buzz in a twinkly high.
I trip and stumble, oh me, oh my,
A dance so wild, I nearly fly!

The world awakens, sleepy and slow,
Nature's canvas with dampened glow.
The sun brings warmth, says, 'Let's go!'
Outrun the dew, it's quite a show!

So prance around as morning breaks,
In every sparkle, laughter wakes.
Maybe avoid the slippery stakes,
And join the dew in merry takes!

Echoes Under the Aged Canopy

Beneath the boughs of wisdom tall,
A mouse asked, 'Did you hear that call?'
The owl hooted, 'No, not at all,
But let's pretend to have a ball!'

Frogs croak band, with flair and style,
Joining in with a cheeky smile.
The trees sway close, they're in denial,
'We're too old for this'—but stay awhile!

Each branch a stage, a leafy crown,
Amidst the giggles, nobody frowns.
The squirrel's antics draw the town,
'Just watch this show!'—with a tiny gown!

In echoes loud, the laughter spills,
Underneath these ancient thrills.
So join the frolic, skip the frills,
In aged glee, we chase the chills!

Under the Cloak of Nature

In the park, a squirrel goes,
Searching for acorns, who knows?
With a leap, it miscalculates,
Bounces off, and contemplates.

The ducks quack a silly tune,
Waddling round like a cartoon.
One dives in, but has no luck,
Comes up wet, a plucky duck.

A breeze blows whispers through the trees,
Tickling leaves, making them tease.
A chipmunk giggles, hides away,
Saying, 'This prank made my day!'

All around, the laughter spills,
Nature's show with funny thrills.
So if you pause and take a look,
You might find joy in every nook.

Beneath the Weight of Time

A turtle moves at a snail's pace,
Complaining 'bout this silly race.
A rabbit hops and laughs, then slips,
Falls right down, and does a flip.

Old trees creak with tales to tell,
Of all the funny things that fell.
A branch once tried to grab some sun,
But ended up on a run **with a bun.**

Clouds drift by in cotton candy,
Changing shapes, oh so dandy.
A lion yawns beneath the sun,
Claims he won, but lost the fun.

Yet time ticks on, as it likes,
With silly winks and funny spikes.
The world laughs in its own sweet way,
Telling us to enjoy today.

The Secret Life of Leaves

Leaves gossip in the gentle breeze,
Whispering tales of clumsy bees.
One flutters down, does a twirl,
And lands atop a drowsy girl.

A leaf, dressed in autumn's glow,
Tries to dance but moves too slow.
It slips and falls, a wibbly flight,
Landing on a cat that takes a fright.

They play hide and seek in the light,
Hiding from squirrels with all their might.
One leaf shouts, 'Catch me if you can!'
But ends up on a puzzled man.

So if you wander where trees bend,
Listen close to the rustle and blend.
Nature's laughter gives a sweet reprieve,
In the antics of the daring leaves.

Hushed Cries of the Wild

In the woods, a fox plays tricks,
Sneaks around with silly flicks.
A wise old owl hoots with glee,
Watching the antics from a tree.

A raccoon tiptoes, thinks he's sly,
But trips on roots, oh my, oh why?
The forest echoes with soft chuckles,
As it witnesses all their struggles.

A bear that sneezes shakes the ground,
Spilling berries all around.
And every critter has a laugh,
At the bear's unplanned berry bath.

So if you wander where they play,
You might just join the fun today.
For in the wild, both meek and mild,
Silly moments go wild and wild.

www.ingramcontent.com/pod-product-compliance
Lightning Source LLC
Chambersburg PA
CBHW051700160426
43209CB00004B/968